When
The
Stars
Dim

-Samantha Rose

To you; Spencer.
My best love, best friend,
and greatest treasure
-love me

The
Confusion

Chapter 1

He told me one thing that makes my heart flutter.

"Forever and ever and always and ever," he said in earlier times. Every moment since, I fell deeper in love with him.

The first moment that I met him, my life seemed to glow and that was something I didn't want to ever lose. I'm very inclined to say that there was always one thing that I knew would be true in my life, him. I never wanted to lose him but, sometimes life gives you situations that leave your heart to skip a beat and others that will break it in half.

I closed the cover of my leather-bound journal and heard the empty sound of tear-stained paper closing together. I never thought once in my life that the pain I was feeling could be so deep. In that moment, my tears kissed the necklace I wore for him, and my eyes closed as I relived every moment I ever knew I fell so deeply in love.

It all started my junior year of High-school at Chino Valley

High-school, there seemed to be something in the air that reflected an ambiance that this might end up good. I didn't know how to react to this new sense of clarity, but it brought a little hope into seemingly gray days after a recent breakup that drained my sense of hope, with someone far too bad for my well-being.

I didn't want to trudge into my first class. Despite it being culinary that didn't seem to make me want to be excited about school. I tried to figure out where I wanted to sit and chose a seat next to a few people that I knew.

After a few days of chatting, and far too much laughter, our teacher decided to sit us with very different people. Luckily enough I seemed to at least know one person I was sitting with.

Although, when I spotted him, someone across from me that I hadn't known, but had seen. I had passed him a couple of times last year after art class and that was to be the end of our encounters. He had medium-dark brown hair, fair skin (but not too fair) and the air of a person quieter than most.

As I was looking at him noticing these things, he then made eye contact with me and for the first time I saw his eyes. I was taken aback by the sheer beauty of them, they were green with a little bit of blue, the darkest blue-gray around the iris and the most stunning color of amber and soon I fell in love with a color of eye that didn't know me yet. I heard his name as the teacher called attendance, Spencer: the name rang in my ears, but I broke contact while resuming the conversation with my friend.

I smiled at my friend apprehensive as all I said was "yeah." Entranced in someone I didn't know.

He was very quiet, smiled at some jokes, but most times, he just kept to himself. There was this reluctance as if I was afraid to know him, but I knew I wanted to.

2 weeks passed by seamlessly, I tried to talk more and more with him, although he still seemed very preoccupied with himself. He would answer shortly, and that was it. In my mind I concluded that Spencer did not like me much, but that soon changed.

It was around the middle of August and today was the first day we actually stepped foot in the kitchen. I remember that day to be the most ground-breaking moment of our friendship.

Our teacher sighed as she waited for everyone to simmer down, "Alright everyone, let's pick partners!"

I then heard the sound of people conversing, knowing that soon everyone would quickly pick the people they knew. We stepped into the culinary room and reveled in the smell of dry flour, and cookies, we then began to learn the first thing we were going to do that day as well as the year. Pies, cookies and more pies seemed to be on the agenda for quite some time. I still didn't have a partner and I had no one to go to, except one person.

Spencer and I looked at each other in sort of a

knowing way.

He shyly looked at me and said "want to be partners?"

I looked at him and smiled at the shyness of this man who was now my friend and I smiled and said "of course!"

The weeks passed, and as we cooked, cleaned and mostly talked it soon became my favorite class that year. I didn't know what it was, but I knew that it had something to do with him. The days I would walk into class sad, happy, mad or weary he seemed to make me laugh endlessly. We could talk about multiple things, and the relationship that was strained from what I had heard from him as we talked more and more.

"She's cheated, she yells

at me for everything and I don't know how to do anything right in his eyes," he told me this with a confused look.

As he told me this a few days before I knew the reluctance from him was warranted. She ultimately told him she was going out with someone else, in fact an ex of hers. Of course, in every sense this should have angered him but his reaction was indifferent,

I held the phone up to my face and I hesitantly asked, "are you okay then?"

Silence came haunting from the other end and I heard the tiredness in his voice as he replied "I don't even care what she does at this moment."

As much as this irritated me I was happy, that meant I

could spend as much time with him as I could. I soon felt my heart drop as my parents told my sister and I we were going out with our cousins. I wanted everything to at least spend time with him. This urgency scared me as if my mind knew I was about to want someone I couldn't have and I didn't know what to do with it.

When we got back to school, the next few weeks he seemed to be in low spirits. I knew he was having a very hard time with his girlfriend. There didn't seem to be anything to cheer him up no matter how much we talked or tried to make him feel better.

It seemed that our teacher came in the best time possible. She came up to me and told me about the event coming up soon for FCCLA. FCCLA is the Family Career and Community Leaders of America, and there are many events you can choose to compete in and from that you can go to events. This year it was FLEX; Fall Leadership Extravaganza, that our teacher really wanted to go to. She said that I could get a feel for the events and the categories that I can compete in. Since I did want to go to state to compete I decided that it would be a great idea to go. I felt though that Spencer should go too. I knew that it would be the best thing for him as well as me. She told me that it was in about a week, that seemed to be a great amount of time to think about. I told Spencer that he should go with us, he seemed to be very reluctant to jump aboard. I told him to think about it, and it would be a good thing to do.

That night I texted him, my palms felt damp and my stomach felt queasy as I texted, "Hey you should go to FLEX!"

My pace quickened as I saw that he was typing back.

"Hey why do you think so? It seems weird that I'm texting you."

It was our first time texting each other, over messenger to say the least but something. I didn't know what was the least bit weird about it but I couldn't possibly know his reasoning. It was more than nice.

After much talking I convinced him that it was just a very fun thing, and he would have a good time, and I wanted him to go.

I didn't know that it would be the beginning of something we didn't expect.

Chapter 2

FLEX, it was around 6 o'clock in the morning and I met everyone at Maverick. I climbed aboard and smiled as he gestured to the spot next to him. I sat down, and we immediately started talking.

"I finally broke up with her" he said this with a soft voice but a slight smile on his face.

I didn't know what to think about this sense of happiness from him, but all I could say was, "wow, I'm glad."

In some odd way it seemed we were the only ones in that bus as our words filled the air with knowing of each other.

I saw the reluctance as he spoke and said, "I guess I'm just annoyed that ever since then she keeps yelling at me for no reason, like I'm still hers."

I sat there contemplating and trying to conjure up the correct words to say, "I think that you just need to tell her off, she's not with you anymore, she needs to accept that."

I saw the slight nod come from him as he smiled at me. The feeling I got in that moment made no sense, he was my friend and slowly almost my best friend. I quieted my thoughts as we continued our ride to the event.

His phone continuously went off during that ride and his mood dropped increasingly. I tried everything for us to keep talking so he would eventually ignore it, it seemed my wish helped. He ignored her texts/calls and boy did his phone go off more than it had before. When got into phoenix, we tried to find our way around and ultimately landed in front of the arena we were supposed to be in. As we climbed out of the bus, our class stood in front of the arena waiting for the doors to open but we had an hour or so, we decided on getting lunch. As we walked down the sidewalk his phone went off and as he read the message his face dropped and he got very upset. I then took his phone and saw the message from his girlfriend Kara, and it was very inappropriate. It entailed that he should just go f*** my Mexican p****.

I then looked at him, shocked even, but I then said with a slight smirk on my face, "okay, first of all, I'm not even Mexican."

I saw his face light up as his face crinkled and he laughed with a gusto I hadn't heard before. I saw this and if even I was telling the truth, I knew if it would give him a laugh, I was glad.

There were multiple places that we could choose from, most chose from panda and or a vegetarian place, Spencer and I decided on getting Five Guys. As it came to be our turn we picked out the same thing, Double cheeseburger, with mayo and tons of mushrooms, as well as some Cajun French fries. As our order got rung up, I placed the money down and he looked at me with awe and a slight smirk on his face. When we went outside, he smiled at me and said, "no-one's ever bought me anything before, it's just nice."

I looked at him and smiled, I didn't know it was a big deal but I knew it was to him. I shrugged and said, "well it's no big deal, I wanted to do it."

The look he gave me expressed a gratitude I didn't understand but knew was deeper than I thought.

The rest of the night was great, we went into the arena, the game started and it was one of the best times I have had in such a long time. Afterwards we spent time going around the workshops. We had a lot of fun and I ended up seeing the group of friends I got close with during camp earlier during the year. We left the arena and went outside to walk around as well as get some dinner before we had to head back home.

Spencer and I ended up choosing a pizza place to eat dinner at. As we went to the back of the line we said to each other that we had to choose something pretty quick. Although, as we worked our way up the line talking, laughing and growing closer together; we didn't get anywhere near choosing. When we got right up to the counter to choose dough and toppings we laughed at each other, telling ourselves

we should have chosen sooner.
We chose to get thin crust
pizza dough with pepperoni and
mushrooms. As we got our pizza
boxed up we headed out toward
the bus to wait for everyone
else.

The night air was filled with
jazz music that came from the
streets and the chatter of
people passing by. We both sat
down on the sidewalk and ate
some of our pizza. As the
music got louder and more
upbeat, I sprung up, looked at
him with a smile of my face as
I said, "let's dance."

He kind of shook his head
with apprehension and said no.

While this he smiled as I started to twirl around. As I was, I didn't know if he knew, but he looked at me with this look I can't begin to try to describe to you. It made the butterflies in my stomach and the longing in my heart for him stronger than before.

The class then started to come back and the bus pulled up to the side of the curb, I really didn't want this day to end but it had to eventually. As we sat on the bus and the teacher took a head count we started our way back home.

As he sat down, I had the pizza in my lap and he seemed to have a million thoughts going on. I didn't know if It was his ex, the night ending or something else. I gave him his phone back which I suppose had quite an impact on his mood. I then wrapped my arms around him and he sort off slumped into them with this sadness and stress that I wish I could squeeze out of him. I told him that we should listen to some calming music and see if that helps, he agreed. The whole way back was great, we talked, listened to music, ate, and just really enjoyed each other's company. As I walked into my house my feelings for him deepened and I knew that he was my best friend, this was all I could have asked for.

The next Monday coming back to

school we were closer than before. Having just broken up with the girl he was with seemed to lift his spirits but she continuously drug him down. Calling every night to yell at him for being horrible to her and not listening to why they should still be together. She continuously got upset that he wasn't trying to work it out. He was drained and he didn't know what to do. I finally just told him to ignore it, he already broke up with her there Is nothing that he could do.

After a few days of doing that he seemed better and I was very glad for that. It was almost veteran's day and we had the day off, it was on a Wednesday which was weird but we weren't complaining. My friend Alyssa came up with the idea that we should go to the Grand Canyon, which we were all very up for. Our teacher then stated that we should go to Bearizona too, it was also going to be free, which she was happy about. Spencer and I were very excited to go, I wasn't all too excited about getting up super early Wednesday morning though.

Wednesday morning came, I got up early with my dad and got dressed as warm as I could. He then drove me to the school to meet up with the few people that were coming along. As I climbed into the van, I smiled as I saw Spencer sitting there with a pillow. I wrapped my blanket around me and I suppose I expected to fall asleep but we couldn't stop talking.

"I didn't know we both loved potatoes so much," he said with a smile on his face.

I looked at him and soon my face matched his.

We spoke of our dreams, our problems, our stress, we laughed, and I never felt more comfortable with someone in my life. He was my best friend and I guess that's the greatest thing I ever wanted.

When we got into Flagstaff, our teacher drove towards the south rim. As we stepped on the snow-covered ground, and into the chill of that morning, I fell in love even more with winter. We made our way towards the rim and just reveled in the beauty.

We all were talking amongst ourselves which a few people there didn't quite like. They soon hushed us so they could revel in God's creation in silence. In that perfect moment our teacher came barreling around the corner talking to us, and as we shushed her, she simply said, "what? Are we having church?" I don't think I've laughed that hard ever,

She shrugged slightly and as her foot went in front of the other she slipped hard.

We started laughing trying to be as quiet as we could, knowing we failed with the glare of strangers on us.

We made our way up to the rim and as the sky began reflect and in between hour of dawn and first light, orange kissed the sky and Spencer and I looked in awe at the beauty that was the sunrise. I don't think time or space was important in that moment, it seemed to whisk away like dew in the first ray of sunshine. I didn't know what that sky was doing, or that day but I looked at him and my heart swelled. I didn't know what it meant but I knew it meant more,soon my mind and most importantly my heart told me he was it, he felt like forever.

Our class started to head down to the village with a café, and cool gift shops. He and I went our way through each one, and found ourselves; every time, immensely alone. Our class then began its way to have breakfast which I am glad for because I was starving, and I'm pretty sure everyone else was too. After a bunch of laughing and pretty good food, the day trudged on. We slowly filed outside, some stayed in the gift shop, some went to the other stores,

Spencer and I found ourselves overlooking a huge part in the Grand Canyon and quite perfectly there was a ledge below the path. We looked over our shoulders quickly and laughed as we swung our legs over the brick wall and climbed our way down to the ledge. It felt slightly dangerous but right. We laid down the blanket that I brought and as we sat down hours seemed to slip by, even though in that infinite moment, only 30 minutes had passed.

His voice cracked slightly as he opened up,

"I don't know I just never fully got over my parents' divorce, I had a hard time, suicidal even, it was even harder when I knew my sister had died. It was too much." I didn't know what to think of this, but my heart broke in that second for him.

I heard the emotion in his voice as he told me all of the deepest most vulnerable parts of his past and the exact emotions he ever struggled with. Talks he had with friends, the promises he had with others. He told me everything inside I could ever hope to know about a person.

He looked me in the eyes and said, "All I care about is what I tell you, and you're the only one I care that knows."

I don't know what went through my mind as he looked into my eyes longer than usual. My mind drew a blank, and all I felt through my veins were the words, and feelings that he was the one. Time seemed to slip through my fingers like sand, and the infinite reality hit me. I didn't know what this meant, and I didn't know what this feeling was, but it was more, so much more than a crush.

After we finished at the Grand Canyon and everyone got what they needed, we headed off to Bearizona. I think the best part was walking around and seeing all the animals that they had. Spencer loved the otters the most, and it was the most surprising thing that I saw. I could see the way his face lit up with happiness over an animal. We walked through all the pathways and talked more and more.

I didn't know I could open up so much to someone before but it didn't feel like it, it felt as if I had already told him all these things. We passed through a gift shop that had interesting things, necklaces, knives, huge dream catchers, paintings and many more. As I looked through the row of necklaces I saw one that seemed to draw my attention more than the rest. Spencer then saw one that he really liked as well, in that moment we decided to get them. We headed towards the van and I suppose that seemed to be the moment I felt it even more.

We stopped at a McDonalds on the way there and his ex-called, I picked it up because he didn't want to. I think I had it coming because she cussed me out like never before. As I sat on the phone for probably longer than it should have been I realized it was the only daunting thing that day, and I'm glad for it.

I got home that afternoon, and I don't know what changed, but I loved him. I understood that the feeling that flew through my mind and was instantly pertinent was that I loved him. I'm in love with my best friend, and I'm not sure where this leaves me. It leaves me with this endless heart pulling at my mind to act upon this newfound clarity, but how could it be so strong so fast?

I want desperately for this to be something beautiful, amazing, loving but there was a huge issue. This friendship that I have with him hasn't been like any I have had with anyone in my life. Realizing that I could truly and fully love my best friend is the best situation anyone could ever hope to be in, I just couldn't mess up the relationship we already had.

This bond so insurmountable that it hurts to not have anything more. I couldn't risk ruining what we already had for something that my heart wants so urgently. I couldn't do that to my best friend, or even my heart for that matter. I just wished that doing this and realizing it wasn't as hard as it has to be. I wish that it was something easier, loving him will either be the best thing that could happen to me or if not, the worst heartache I'll ever have to experience in my life.

Chapter 3

The glimmer of hope that seemed to come through when we came back the next day seemed to diminish quickly. Spencer and I sat in our zero-hour Spanish class, and Kara came through the door angrily she lightly whispered to us, "can I talk to you guys outside?"

I rolled my eyes because why does this have to be a thing when they are not together anymore. Spencer and I looked at each other and followed begrudgingly behind her. When we got outside, she looked him straight in the eye and said

"Why would you do that to me?"

He looked taken aback and

I think that I probably looked the same. I couldn't believe that even after they broke up she still felt it was pertinent that Spencer should treat her the same as when they were together. I remember looking into his eyes and seeing a sense of irritation while trying to be nice. She then went on to call him names, and I quote

"How can you be such an asshole, jerk, and cunt."

I looked at him and he seemed unfazed and he replied slowly, and clearly

"Well which one is it?"

I put my hand over my mouth trying not to show the smile and chuckle that came out. To know that there was such a long time that he would never stick up for himself because of not wanting to fight and hurt anyone, I was proud to look at him and see a newfound confidence for himself. She didn't like it much though. As she looked him in the face clearly hurt she just simply said

"All of them."

After this I sort of tuned it all out because as she kept bickering to him, calling him names, and furious beyond belief, we finally ended it and headed back into class.

I know that this was his ex, but that was the point, it was his ex. Nothing made sense about what she was doing, but I didn't want to spend the time to figure it out.

Today marks a day where we haven't been having to deal with the cruel way of his ex. She seemed to rely heavily on making it a skeptical in front of as many people as she could. All he wanted was to leave it cleanly and as painless as possible for her sake as well as his. That seemed to be the furthest way of doing things in her mind, which not only was aggravating him but me as well. It was a constant battle and a battle with me being involved.

It is now the end of November and for the past week Spencer has been apologizing for bringing me into this mess of a breakup. You see, I don't even mind it because all I want is for him to be happy and if I could provide some sort of happy than I want to stay even if being his friend cost me being ridiculed by a girl not over a breakup. I didn't know why I was putting up with it but I knew he was worth it and more.

We sat in zero-hour Spanish talking about the things we were going to make in culinary which we were both beyond excited for. As our group was talking and trying not to get discouraged about Spanish. Kara stepped in the class and shoved a box of stuff in his face and left. All of us looked at each other quite perplexed about what just happened. I looked at him and he looked even more done than the day before. I didn't know what to do, I honestly didn't but I knew she wasn't doing anything to make it better, I was just hoping this would be the end of it. Quite unfortunately I am to be surely mistaken.

Spencer and I walked into the art room because of a poster we had to do for FCCLA. It was very hard because she was in there, and she didn't seem to want to leave us alone. We tried our best to ignore her which I was pretty proud of. As him and I walked out of the classroom she looked us straight in the eye and in the fakest voice I have ever heard, she said,

"Bye, have a nice day you guys!"

Usually I would've have left it alone but I was very fed up and I suppose I was done trying to be nice to her so I simply shouted back,

"Fuck you Kara."

Spencer and I then walked out of the classroom not really wanting or caring to try to see her reaction. He seemed to be on the edge of his patience and I didn't blame him at all.

December, the time of the year that him and I are quite excited because this is our favorite time of the year. The

chill in the air, lights glowing and the smell of pumpkin and peppermint was the ultimate happiness for us. We didn't know what the next year would hold but I knew it had to be something better than what we were having to deal with.

For the past few days Spencer was trying his hardest to give Kara the things she asked for back. It seemed to be the most impossible task in the world, the minute he would try to go up to her she would walk away without a care in the world. Today was his last day of putting up with it and so was I. It was the 6th of December and it seemed like any ordinary day. School was quite boring for us and we were looking forward to Christmas break coming up soon. We walked towards the buses because my best friend Elizabeth wanted to talk. Spencer tried his best all day to give her things back but it seemed to be the same endless cycle of stubbornness. He looked at me exasperated and breathed out,

"I don't know what to do, I don't want to carry her shit around anymore. I've tried."

I looked at his face of impatience and tiredness, I then decided that this was the last time this would be a problem. I then stated that he should maybe just get rid of it if she clearly doesn't want it as much as she had said before. As we passed by a trash can he just set it on top of it, he then called her and said,

"Look I've tried to give your stuff back and you won't take it back so it's in the trash if you want it."

I know that to any normal person that would be beyond rude but this was the most plausible thing in our situation. The pain and hurt that she was causing and didn't seem to care about was just about enough for him. I didn't want him to go through anything like this anymore, because he didn't deserve anything as low as this.

Spencer, Elizabeth and I were talked amongst ourselves, having a good time. I then looked in my peripheral and saw Kara storming towards us. I didn't know what was coming until she threw a punch at Spencer. It was all so fast and as I saw him guard his face, I got livid. I then got in the middle trying to stop her from hitting him. I then yelled,

"Stop touching him!"

She then stopped, quite calmly and said,

"oh, you want me to touch you?"

In my head I kept saying, I don't care at least it's not him and man does this bitch deserve it. The next thing I heard was his voice saying as he got between us and put his hands out were the words,

"oh, no you don't"

I didn't know what happened in that instance but my heart beat faster. I looked at him and the feeling I felt was beyond describable. I didn't know what was fully happening to me, but I knew I didn't want to not have him in my life.

The drama teacher and a few of her students came out and of course she automatically threw her hands up, stating for him to not touch her. I have never seen such fire in Spencer's eyes as he yelled,

"She hit me!!!!"

As we all got escorted to the principals' office the indication that everyone was running by was that, Spencer had hit her. I sat through the questioning of what happened and the drama teacher simply stating that I must like to hit people. My mind began to come up with so many different things to say to defend myself, but it seemed to be useless. As they sent me out of the office I then went to the Cross country teams coach classroom where my sister was waiting. I came in livid because no one was believing Spencer and me. I was retelling this story to my sister Sandra, I looked through my phone and in a miraculous way I had gotten the whole thing on video. I didn't know how or when, but I jumped out of my seat and walked as quickly as I could to the principal's office. I quickly ran into his office and told them that I had gotten the incident on video. Events seemed to turn around quickly after they saw the real story.

Spencer and I walked out of the principal's office, a

little mad but relieved. Not
only did that help our case
but it helped them see that
she wasn't as innocent as she
laid out. She ended up getting
suspended for a few days or so
which helped Spencer in so
many ways that I didn't know
internally but could plainly
see on his face.

Chapter 4

The rest of the month seemed to drag on a little but only because he started to talk to a girl in his class. Of course, I was happy for him but in my mind, I was not. I was unhappy, I didn't like it. I couldn't do anything about it and it bothered me even more that I couldn't, even though I was only his best friend. Her name is Emily and she is actually pretty nice, but not right for him. I could tell but I didn't want to say anything even though secretly I did.

He was so much better than she was and I didn't have to spend tons of time with her to know that. As the few weeks seemed to drag on quite slowly

I actually started to talk to a friend of his, something was happening between us. It seemed wrong because of the way I felt about Spencer, but there was nothing I could do about not being able to fully have Spencer.

It all started one-day, downtown Prescott and at a festival for Christmas. The town held it every year mostly for people to play music, have hot chocolate and cookies.

Spencer and I went because our culinary teacher asked if we would like to help some people hand out cookies. We agreed because if it was

something for us to hang out
and something fun, we would.
Mostly though, because it had
to do with Christmas time.
Spencer gushed continuously
about the happiness that
Christmas brought him. It
reminded him of times with
grandparents and the times his
family was together still. It
reminded him of home. Also, it
was our favorite time of the
year coincidently enough. It
was December 11th and we were
very much looking forward to
it.

Spencer and I arrived downtown
around 4:30, we strolled
downtown and inevitably
decided to get some hot

chocolate. His friend whose name is Cole wanted to hang out with us because he was going to be there. We then said that we could meet up for dinner. We had dinner with Cole and his grandma. It was actually really fun, and it was nice to spend time with one another. We headed to the business we were supposed to help hand out cookies with. We were running around, laughing, smiling and joking around. It seemed though that Spencer had a problem with the fact that Cole and I were laughing and having fun, I guess you could say we were flirting. I didn't really notice but I didn't mind.

Spencer was starting to talk to someone and to me it was useless to try be strung up on someone I could never have, so I said to myself. If it did happen between his friend and I, I wouldn't be too mad about it.

The night went on and we went around antique stores, watched a few people throw some fire around, bought some books and walked around the Christmas lit square. The night ended and it was honestly really great.

Spencer and I got into his truck and there was an awkward silence. I didn't know what to do about it or even address it. I then asked him what was wrong and if he was mad or upset at me. He just looked at me and slightly smiled and said,

"No, no I just don't know what we are going to do."

I looked at him for what felt

like hours, he didn't seem to understand that I felt the same way. It also was hard because he was interested in someone else, it just seemed useless. As he drove on to my house I just started the conversation, I believe we both had dreaded or even were afraid. I then said

"Look, I know you're talking to someone and you might want to be with her and It's just hard because I'm afraid of what could happen between us."

He looked at me and nodded his head in agreement. Quite honestly, I don't remember all of what was exactly said, but I knew it was mostly that we didn't want to ruin our friendship. Throughout the conversation I knew that we both hated the predicament because more is what we knew we wanted with each other.

When I got home, got ready for bed and sat in my room, I guess I was upset. Upset, because the thing I think we wanted the most was something we could never cross the line to get to. How does any sane person live with that as reality?

The next few weeks passed by slowly it was painfully true that both of us were aware of something else between us. He was dating Emily now and it seemed unfair, I didn't know why I felt like this but it was an issue. Although I had been talking to Cole for the last few weeks as well. I suppose I liked it but I didn't know in what way. Spencer seemed to have a bittersweet response to it. He really didn't like it but he knew that he couldn't have any other reaction. I believe that somewhere deep inside of us there was something that we both wanted but ignored, cast away, and laughed off. I loved him and I didn't know if he loved me but I knew there was something more.

The month passed by quickly and January came to be, Cole and I started to date which changed things but not by much. We were as close as ever but the prospect of another in our lives created unease. We had a talk about this whole situation before his friend or I even started dating, his main concern was how he would treat me. The conversation that resulted was this,

He said, *"Ahh, would you date him, this is just my curiosity I wouldn't tell him what you say?"*

As I read this text I didn't know what to say, but I continued the conversation,

I replied, *"I'm not sure, I feel like even if I would it would depend on time. I know you wouldn't, and if you did I wouldn't mind, but I feel like you would be upset if I ever did."*

Spencer then replied,

"That's understandable, honestly I would probably be jealous to some degree and irritated but I guess it's whatever. I don't want him to fuck you over or anything either. One other thing I guess too is that whenever I feel you like him and I start to "compete" or something like that I just want to give up because I know I couldn't beat him. I know that's probably a shitty thing to say but yeah, I don't want to have to compete for someone again, it just doesn't work out well."

In going through this conversation, it not only made me slightly upset but also sad. I loved him so much and, in a heartbeat, he could beat out his friend because he was the one I loved. The only thing that held this opportunity back is his girlfriend. I didn't want to jeopardize his relationship as well as ours. In this instance I knew nothing could be done about it as much as I wanted it. I did really like his friend and in that liking, I knew that it could be something. I knew that there was nothing I could do but I knew that Cole and I both want a relationship, what's the harm in that?

I knew for Spencer that there was nothing wrong with it, but deep down he wanted something, why would he have acted out the way that he did?

Chapter 5

The times throughout the month seemed to slip by seamlessly, but painfully. There was something about having significant others in our lives that seemed wrong. I didn't know what to do, I didn't know how to react to it. Emily was honestly very nice at least in the beginning, she didn't like me after a while which I understand in some way. Spencer talked deeply with me more than her.

Spencer looked at me with unease and with a sad voice said, "I don't know it's just frustrating because I care about her but I don't enjoy talking with her. She answers short and its always the same thing. I don't know I guess that's why I just enjoy talking to you so much."

In every part of my heart I wanted to tell him to break it off, to not put up with it but his happiness with her was more important. I softly replied, "just talk to her about it and it should be fine."

Also, Cole, he was very fun to be with but I'm not sure if I understood what it was that was between us. There was a connection but I didn't know if it was anything close to romantic. The borderline feelings between Spencer and I seemed to grow stronger and stronger as our relationships went on but never verged further for us. We both didn't know what to think of it but it was something. There was a feeling between us that showed itself the day at the Grand Canyon and since then I've been fighting it. I don't know if he was but I liked to believe he did.

It was the middle of January and everything seemed to be going great, or so I would like myself to believe. I had this prepositioned thought in my head that I loved Cole. I didn't know if it was for getting out of a relationship a year back and finally having a romantic connection with someone, or if it was the urgent feeling I got when I began to recognize the love I had for Spencer. I would like to believe it was because I honestly did, but no, that just wasn't it. Cole talked to me, he laughed with me, he complimented me, he held my hand, he kissed me, he did all these things you're supposed to do but it wasn't enough. That fateful Acker night where it was carefree, flirtatious, intention was there. It was beautiful but perhaps not in the way I'm thinking. The late night talks we have and the long calls of meaningful, goofy insights were just what I need. It's what I crave for, someone to honestly, totally be aware. The question I ask myself; is why is there something missing?

Everything was great, I am happy, I am honestly good but why is it hesitant. Why? Perhaps this thought came to be because Spencer is with someone but that just didn't seem like enough justification. He constantly told me of the way that he could never talk to her. He could never feel happy around her if not only for a brief moment. He couldn't be who he was and it baffled me that with me it was totally and undeniably him. He told me that being with her was just being with someone sad. He felt so bad for her and wanted to help but it wasn't enough for him, he needed more. He texted me continuously that he loved talking with me and felt bad for not feeling the same about her. It seemed so pure, so innocent, but it got everything in me rising to the surface.

There was something about

him being with her that I
didn't like. I didn't want
this thought to be true, but I
knew it had to be.

As my window filled with the
dim of orange and yellow hue
of morning light, I looked
outside and it seemed
perfectly still. The morning
breathed in the innocent form
of a new day and I knew what
this confusion had to be. I
walked into the culinary room
doors, and the look I saw on
his face, and I bet was on
mine too, revealed a tune so
true. There was something, but
I turned my head away from
him, and shielded away the
form growing more in my heart.

I could not possibly feel something like this for him when I am with Cole, its wrong but for some reason it didn't feel like it. Cole and I were doing fine, there was a bond, we could talk and seeing each other at school which helped in the end. The only thing is that the conversations were great but didn't bring a feeling, other than appreciation. I liked him very much, but I didn't know if it was in the way we both wanted it to be.

Now, Emily and Spencer, they were still dating and they seemed fine, but the way he told me constantly that it was so depressing to be with her. She wanted a way out of her normal life when she was with him, but there wasn't a lot that he even wanted to do.

It was hard for him when he didn't really like her family at all, and it was hard being with her when it was constant sadness engulfing her and him. It seemed that this was a recurrent issue in their relationship and I wished so badly it would end. I knew that I had no control over it no matter how much I needed it to be. The times of this worry and ache seemed to be endless and quite frankly I had enough of loving someone I could never have. Besides he cared for her and I cared for Cole, extremely. Just what was the problem with my make-believe feelings that I tried desperately to inflict upon this relationship. The problem was that, I needed this new sense of clarity if not even a sense of comfort.

Cole was beyond what I thought in the beginning, as I loved him in a friend way and because of that I began to reflect that I loved him romantically and it's been ultimately messing with everything I believe in, True love. As we got into a relationship everything about him changed, to me it seemed that the effort was no longer there, the way he cared was just as pertinent but the effort of keeping me didn't seem close in his mind. I suppose it's just something in my head.

It was the beginning of February and I was ready for

the months to get closer to the end of the year as well as valentine's day. Valentine's day was never a huge thing on my mind ever but somehow, I thought that this time it would ultimately be way different than I conjured in my head. It was February 6th my two very great friends, Rosio and Micalyn wanted to hang out and I was up for it 100%. As we went out downtown, messed around and made complete fools of ourselves it was the best time that I had with girlfriends in a very long time. We were sitting in pizza hut having pasta, and talking about boys, life, and school I then decided to call Cole. As I called him, I couldn't talk for long but from there I didn't know what to think of it. It's not that I didn't like talking to him but it didn't sit right with me anymore. As the night went on and we finally got home I lay in bed that night contemplating what I was actually doing.

I didn't know if it was the same for Cole, or if I was going crazy but for the next couple of days he seemed to ignore me. I would go up to him as he talked to his friends and he would just smile vaguely at me and walk away. The disappointment that hit my soul was deep and I didn't know what to do about it. The next day I woke up to a text that spurred up anxiety. It was a text from him saying essentially that we really needed to talk about our relationship because he was not happy where it was going. I remember thinking in that instance that it could be something easily solved, well I thought.

That day was the same as before he ignored me endless times and all I wanted was to talk to him about this issue. I talked that day to Spencer many times about it and he didn't know what to think of it other than that he didn't like it very much.

The end of the day came quickly and as I walked out of my class ready to go finish my Spanish test, he approached me. I stood still in front of him, frozen for what may or may not be coming up and the latter became the result. He said that he really couldn't do it anymore, it wasn't going anywhere, we didn't hang out and it just wasn't working out. In the forefront of my brain I started to come up with all these things to counteract the things that was prevalent on his lips, and it stopped.

In the back of my mind something was telling me to let it happen, that it just didn't need to be a fight or attempt of saving. The words that slipped out of my mouth were that, there was nothing I could do and that I respect his decision. He nodded and kind of smiled and walked away. In that moment I felt hurt, sad, but in a weird way totally okay. I sort of sat down and in any break up I cried, but it stopped. I looked at my phone and immediately called Spencer, I just had to tell him because there was nothing I wouldn't tell him. As it came off my lips and I heard his voice resonate back through the phone I suddenly felt totally and completely okay.

This breakup didn't matter as much to me as much as it mattered to me that I had to talk to him, I had to hear his voice in such a comforting way. The next few days, were a little hard because of the way I had to see him, but talking, cooking, and laughing with Spencer seemed to make that hardness worth it.

Chapter 6

The next weeks seemed to pass by like the breeze on a spring day; brief, intoxicating and warm. It didn't seem that I had gone through a break up at all, it didn't even seem hard in the least bit. It seemed that I was in the same state I was before we had even dated. The only person I suppose can ever take credit for that is Spencer. In the moments I questioned the ability and beauty of myself he reassured me in any way that he could. In the times I would hear of the hurtful things Coles' friends conjured up ways of why we had broken up, Spencer hugged me in a way that squeezed the hurt out of my soul. I didn't know how I deserved such a best friend,

such an amazingly beautiful,
caring soul that gave so much.
I didn't know how but I knew
that I would never give it up.
In this turmoil beauty came
through and he was it, he was
the reason.

I heard the noise of students
all around me in the cafeteria
and I jumped up at the sight
of a new person walking in.
Spencer had not come to lunch
and I was worried.

"Hey where are you?"

"are you okay?"

*"are we going to have lunch
together?"*

My worry shot like a bullet as my texts were left unread. It was not like him to not answer.

I felt my heart beat faster as I saw his face through the windows and a slight smirk on his face as he walked in the door. I looked at him and there was question in my eyes, he looked at me and handed me a paper. It had a few classmates from his senior class and my head could only decipher the numbers popping up. I slowly looked up and a smile crept on my face, his face lit up

"I'm valedictorian!!"

My eyes lit up and the same wide smile met our faces as we celebrated in his accomplishment. I didn't know I could feel so much happiness

and feel so proud of him than
I did in that moment, I didn't
want it to ever go away.

The two months that have
passed, have been the most
confusing ride of my life.
Ever since that day Cole broke
up with me, even more
importantly the Grand Canyon,
it changed everything. It
changed not only in my mind,
but in my heart, soul and
eyes, he changed. He changed
me. The past two months of
growing closer than we ever
have been which I never
thought was possible. Him
going through a relationship
with Emily that he was never
tuned into.

The hardest part of it all was that the person that helped me the most was just my best friend. It hurt me that he didn't honestly love this person he was with, he wasn't loving the possibility of more with her. It hurt me that he wasn't in the moment he should be in. I didn't know how many nights I spent talking with him, loving him more each day only to wake up the next day as the stars laughed at my dreams of what wouldn't be. It was hard to hear him talk of how much he cared about her and just wanted her to know he would do anything for her. I didn't know if I was selfish or in denial of being so in love. I didn't know how much more my heart could handle of being just his best friend.

I sat in my room my heart quivering and a smile to my ears as I read the heartfelt message from him,

"I'm just so lucky because we can talk about anything and you understand me and you don't judge. I'm just so glad we are lucky to have each other, you're truly my best friend."

I tried to settle the pulsing in my chest and I smiled because it was close, so close.

It just turned to be May, and as the end of the school year approached things were close to the moment I could call him mine and I only hoped I wouldn't be a fool to think so. In the past months since my break up, things between Spencer and I only intensified even with the ever-lingering prospect of his relationship. I tried to beat down the flame inside my heart and just as I thought this was bound to be the heartache of my life, he changed everything, he changed the way I viewed the way he felt about me. It all happened this afternoon the 1st week of May and this is how it played out-

It was a bright sunny afternoon, far too hot for my taste but it could have been worse. Spencer and I chose to hang out today after school so I could go spend time with his animals. This was the most innocent, the pure nature of our relationship. Yes, this had happened before but the feeling I got from this was entirely different. It was something more in his eyes, intensified even more than the growing embers that started that day at the Grand Canyon. It was strange to see this but I didn't question it.

I climbed into his truck and as we went down the road toward his house from the library, the tune of our favorite song played and, in that instance, he held my hand. I sort of froze because I didn't know what I was going to do. What did this mean? Could it mean what I think? Could this be more? All these thoughts raced through my brain and my brain stilled as he looked into my eyes and said

"Is this okay."

In that sweet sound of his asking and the urgency in his eyes I said of course. I didn't know how this was okay, I didn't know if this made me a bad person, but it didn't matter. Nothing mattered. As I felt the warm of his hand and the fit of it in mine it didn't matter that this might not be anything more than I wished for. It didn't matter but that split second of clarity. I don't know what this is going to do, I don't know what this means for us, but it's worth everything good or bad.

"I know I can't fix it."

The words seemed to jump out at me against the white bright of my phone screen. The words I were seeing were hard to read, were sad. I didn't know how to react, how to feel but I knew it was sadness, I just felt sorry for him. I didn't know that this relationship he was in was for sure not going anywhere.

To back it up a little, this started a few weeks ago when he really started talking about him and Emily.

"I don't know it's the same, we can't talk like you and I, all she wants is someone to cling onto because of her family. She's just too sad and barely ever listens to what I need and think."

I felt like I couldn't try to convince him to try, because it didn't seem worth salvaging. I sighed slowly and typed out what I honestly thought.

"well I think you obviously have a problem with how she talks to you, besides this has been a problem for a while now, I don't know if it's going to change. I think you need to really consider things."

After this I didn't know what to think but I went to bed that night hoping he would listen.

The next days seemed to go by fine, the closer it got to be the end of school, the air filled with angst and excitement. It was May 9th, the day was more than bright, it was shining. The sun was bright, warm and happy. The day started off in a way I didn't expect. The other night spencer told me that he couldn't be with Emily anymore, he told her and he hoped it was all okay. I didn't know If I was sorry or happy, I didn't know how I felt and, in the moment, it didn't matter to me which one it had to be.

"I don't know Sam, it was so weird because in the morning she just came and held my hand. I had to tell her it was over but it was just awkward."

From what I heard from that instance it didn't bode that well with her. I suppose I felt somewhat bad but it didn't really matter that much to me. I tried my hardest to let this feeling be a little more sympathetic but I couldn't no matter how much I tried. I loved him, she loved him, and I didn't know how he felt. I could feel it in his stare, I could see it in his laugh, but I didn't know exactly what it meant.

Chapter 7

It was an ordinary day like any other, there was the constant stir of people around me as they waited for class to start. It was almost 8:20 and Spencer was nowhere in sight. I was beyond confused, him and I were always the first ones there and there have been many a time we just talked or bonded over the joy of coming in early and cooking breakfast together.

I slightly shrugged off the annoyance of him not being there and waited to see him come in. Alyssa and I went and got breakfast and as I walked through the door I saw him standing there. I didn't know what to think, but I was happy to see him, I knew that.

Culinary seemed to drag on for what seemed like an eternity, we went into the kitchen and we didn't make anything we could have which was a complete bummer but being in the kitchen eased the havoc in my mind.

I knew that Spencer has been talking to this girl in his Spanish class, I knew her slightly but not too well. He never brought her up only to say that he had started to talk to her, and that's the last thing I heard about her. Her name is Megan and even though I didn't know her, I knew that this would cause a problem. If he was talking to her what were the constant talks and worries of Spencer and I being together for. Did they mean anything at all to him, or was it a ploy to make me hopeful? I hoped in some way that this was just a phase and somehow Spencer could understand that we should just take the plunge. I was mortified of losing him as my best friend if there was more, but it wasn't as bad as watching him care for another in a way that I wanted. It wasn't as bad as sitting home every night wishing for something that might ruin everything we shared. If it wasn't that bad, why was I scared to admit that to him.

Culinary was finally over and the amount of happiness I felt as Spencer and I walked out of the classroom and he talked to me, I couldn't describe. Soon that happiness dissipated, Spencer looked at me as I got ready to head to math, I saw Megan in the distance walking towards us and my hopes fell. My mind went blank as I heard him say,

"I wanted to tell you something and I knew I should tell you myself but Megan and I kissed this morning."

He stared into my eyes for what felt like eternity and reality slipped from my grasp and I just stared at him hurt. I could see that in his eyes he knew something was wrong but before anything else could further on, I walked away to my class. I looked behind me and as he looked at me his gaze went from me to her as she came up. I turned around and went quickly into my Math class getting ready for the test that I had to take. I quietly went outside to do my test, and a tear slipped down my cheek as I stared into the bright sky all around me.

As I stared at the numbers in front of me, it didn't seem too important. I stared at my phone as I saw a text from him, going on as always. I tried to fight the irritancy that came with the hurt but I failed.

"I have your jacket do you want it back?"

In every part of my brain, I felt rude, but in every part of my heart I knew I needed to protect myself from unbearable hurt. In understanding that I understood this was going to be something with her, and I needed to back off as much as

I hated the prospect of doing so. The conversation went on, and the undeniable worry in his texts came through. He was confused, mad at himself, and understanding. I didn't know I could be so hurt, but not mad at the same time. As much as I was upset he couldn't make me keep going on with this mad feeling toward him.

It was around lunchtime and we talked and talked over text, and as much as I kept trying to be mad, to be upset I finally gave in.

"I'm going to go to the nurse because I don't feel good."

My heart hurt because I knew this was because of the hurt going on between us. This spoken but denied thing between us came to light.

There's this fire in my heart now as I recognize that he wants more but denies it. I don't know how this is going to play out but please don't let me lose him forever.

I moved over and Spencer sat next to me, I looked at him with his head down and my throat closed as I knew why he hurt so much. I knew as he told me it was probably nothing it was because of the way I was hurt and told him why. The most I could do at that moment was ask if he was okay and or needed anything. He shook his head no and my spirits drifted further down. I looked into his eyes as we stood up to go to class, and his look revealed more than I thought. His downcast look explained a hurt and love, I didn't know could possibly be there. Of course, over the months I knew there was something more but I didn't know it was just as strong as mine. I smiled at him as he softly asked me

"Is it okay if we still hang out after school?"

I of course agreed, even reluctantly but knew it was something we had planned and needed. I reluctantly walked away from him to my class, and it seemed like it was hours long. The day went on and we hardly spoke, and when we did, it was nothing like before.

My heart slowly drowned in the possibility of losing him

over something I couldn't control but knew would affect us. I know that he is not mine to be jealous and so upset over but, in a way, it felt like he was. All these months of being best friends, with a bond and connection I have never felt before seemed to draw this imaginary chain around us. I didn't know what to do with it and I didn't know how to stop it without breaking this chain and or pulling it tighter, especially now, but I knew I had to do something, we had to.

The
Stars

Chapter 8

It was the end of the school day and as I walked up to Spencer I felt my breath catch in my throat and my heart pound in my chest. I didn't know why I was so worried, we always talked about things, but my heart and brain knew this time was different.

My sister's track banquet is today and I knew we had a limited time so we walked to his truck. I felt the tension and sadness between us and I didn't know what to do about it. As the road stretched before us, the movement that came closer to his house seemed to give me even more anxiety. We pulled into his driveway and he seemed to want to get out but I stayed where

I was. He looked at me confused but I knew this was the time. I looked at him, shyly even, and I asked him,

"why did you do it when we've been talking about us?"

He responded, "I didn't know, I just didn't know us being together was an option."

My head spun with the response that I could possibly say to this and even the fact that he didn't know that it has been. I wanted to say that it might not especially because of her, but it didn't feel right. I only hoped that he knew despite being my best friend I didn't think this would ruin our friendship. My brain didn't even get the chance to register what the next words were but suddenly,

"It's always been an option

Spencer."

I stared blank face at him, not knowing if he knew I didn't even understand what I said. I thought for sure that he was going to react a certain way, or let me down because of Megan but the next thing I saw surprised me indefinitely. His eyes softened and he smiled the most endearing smile I have ever seen him give to me. My heart melted as it finally understood that he felt the way I have this whole time. I didn't know what to say, I didn't even know what to do but I knew from here on out it couldn't get any more confusing. He kept looking at me and as we kind of smiled at each other we agreed that everything was okay, because essentially it was all a misunderstanding.

This denied thing wasn't
denied anymore, we knew that
and it didn't get any better
than that. We both got out of
his truck and I immediately
started to pet his dog Scotty.
He was a cute miniature
Aussie, and I couldn't get
enough of him. We walked in
the front door and was
immediately greeted by his cat
Homer. I have been to his
house a couple of times, but
even still I couldn't get
enough of his pets. I walked
around his house for a few
minutes holding his cat and I
looked at him and there was
something there in his eyes

that I couldn't really read that well.

"Hey I built that plane metal earth model, want to see it?" he asked me with severe question in his eyes.

"yeah of course."

It was my first time seeing his room and it was messy, full of plane models and jeep posters. I walked over to all his models to check out and it was interesting. I saw the intricacies and small details and I couldn't understand how he had the patience for it. It was impressive though, more so he was. I then sat on his bed as I fiddled with the plane model he had.

His face had a strained look and he hesitantly sat next to me and asked, "Are we okay?"

I looked at him and sort
of smiled and there were a lot
of things I wanted to say to
him, but all that could come
out of my mouth were the words
were "Of course we are."

I placed my hand on his
and laid back and closed my
eyes, the only thing I was
thinking in this moment was
that I needed to really think
about what I needed from this
friendship. I suddenly felt
his arm around me and the heat
from his breath next to my
cheek. I didn't open my eyes,
I didn't question him, all I
needed was this moment, and
this moment only. I felt his
lips against my cheek, and I
didn't know what to do, but I
knew I needed it. I looked
over at him and his eyes were
boring into mine and I didn't

know how to feel, I then kissed his cheek softly and the smile that went on our lips was indescribable.

I looked into his eyes and the warmth I felt in my heart was overfilled, slowly and unknowingly our lips crashed together. It was soft, and in a way, that was now known. This feeling that has been between us for the long previous months was ignited. I didn't know what to think, I didn't even know how to respond but to reciprocate back fully. It was slow, nothing sexual, just soft and meaningful. I felt my heart reach out to his, and I felt the soft tingle in my fingertips, when his hand held my face. I felt the calm, and rightness of it all, the "giddy" feeling everyone feels

when they think they're in
love, wasn't there. It wasn't
because I didn't love him but
because I truly loved him. He
was strong, patient, loving,
kind, caring, lovable, smart
and most of all he was safety.
In the moment of our lips
crashing together I felt at
home, he was my home and
that's how I knew I truly
loved this guy. Truly loved my
best friend.

May 20th, May 20th, May 20th, I
could not stop repeating that
in my head as I got ready to
go out with Spencer. Our first
actual date, Our first day as
actual partners. It was
surreal. I didn't know how to

think of it other than listen to the giddiness in my stomach and the warmth I felt in my heart. I tried with all my might to try to conjure up an explanation as to why we hadn't before but nothing ever seemed to make sense. I didn't know why but it didn't matter, because now I had him, officially had him. How could I ever try to question when I had him, I couldn't be selfish with this.

I saw the glint of his car pull in my driveway and my smile pulled to my ears. We were going to dinner at his moms' and stepdads. I could officially meet her and I had been wanting to ever since I became his best friend. As we got to her house it was seamless, we had fun, we finally had something worth everything in the world. As I looked around at him talking to his mom, and I saw the way his face lit up when he said certain things, or the way his laughed filled his face with happiness and I don't think anything could ever get better than this moment right now. This moment of perfect bliss with the one I love with everything I have.

Chapter 9

It's a few days before Graduation for Spencer, who knew I would feel more nervous than he seemed. I didn't know how he felt but I knew he would do great. His speech was after the salutatorian and the co valedictorian. The days leading up to graduation were an exciting time, he was happy, nervous, and mostly ready to get it done. The day before they had a rehearsal and ever since then I was beyond giddy for it to happen. I knew that he would do great and I was beyond ready to see my best friend graduate.

We started dating a few days ago, I know that so many things happened before but it was the perfect moment. In the few days of school we have tried to keep it between us knowing that soon we would be done with school and then everyone didn't have to worry about us. We were a topic amongst my friends, his, and weirdly enough, some teachers. They even talked about us dating, even prior before anything happened, we shrugged it off denying it, and now we know how that worked out.

It was chalk it up day for art and my best friend Elizabeth and I are stoked. All day we have been sitting outside the school and drawing. Yes, we went into some classes but it was relaxing to not have to especially if we could draw instead. Spencer and I were trying to keep it on the down low, but whenever I would see him, my heart would fill up with happiness and the crinkle that formed in my cheek when I smiled was more prominent than ever. We went to our Culinary class to go see if our teacher could sign our yearbook and of course she said yes. We walked into the room and when we got up to her desk, she looked at us and said,

"Finally,"

Spencer looked at me with bewilderment and my eyes met his with the same shock. How could she have known? She was there with the fights with Kara, the times we cooked before class, the unknown between us, she taught the class where I met and fell in love with my best friend, so I suppose her knowing isn't weird at all. We then left her classroom and eagerly waited for the day to end, I smiled because my life was better than I could have ever imagined it to be.

The morning seemed to turn into day quicker than I thought and when the sunlight hit my face that morning of Graduation my heart leaped. The butterflies I felt for him didn't go away and I could not wait for the day to end so that I could see my best friend. He didn't seem to be too worried, but he spent the night before finally writing his Valedictorian speech and it was nerve racking for me and even more so for him. As the day went on in school I quite literally couldn't pay attention to anything other than the fact that he was going to be there and the immeasurable way I felt about this moment for him was more than I ever knew I would feel.

"Hey meet me in the back of the auditorium, all the seniors are supposed to be here, so I guess I have to be here too."

It was towards the back of the building and as I walked through those double doors, I felt excitement and nerves run through my stomach. I felt the anticipation and smile spread across my face as I saw him walking up. It felt surreal, amazing and true.

I could see his face and everything made sense and, in that moment, we wrapped our arms around each other. I didn't know how to feel, other than proud. It's in that moment I knew I couldn't do any better than this and it was absolutely okay.

I saw his face filled with anticipation and panic because he had to speak but I was so proud that he gets this chance to show everyone the kind of person he really is if they hadn't known before. As he walked around to backstage and as I made my way to my seat all I wanted was to jump for joy but wouldn't that look weird?

As I made my way to the seats that my friends decided would be a good place to sit. If only they knew it was farther away from him than I hoped it would be. As I sat down I could see the stage but it seemed light years away. I didn't know what to feel at that moment, but the butterflies shot straight up my stomach and out of my mouth and in its place, I formed a smile so big as I saw him walking to his seat

As the music chimed down, and the chatter quickly dissipated and the rows of Graduates filed out the ceremony started. There were a lot of things that I didn't know I could ever feel as I saw him fidget in his seat, or the way he looked down at the floor, nervous and psyched all in the same emotion. As I heard his name be called to receive his diploma my smile grew and my heart beat faster with every step that he took. He grabbed his diploma and smiled for a picture and a tear came rolling down my cheek, not wanting to be apprehensive for the feelings that kept surfacing in my heart for him anymore. The rest of the names were called and I blurred them out to radiate only his face in the center.

When the end of the ceremony came to be my heart beat faster like the beating of a drum and the ache in my hands to hold his became more apparent. I watched him climb up the stairs and sit in his chair waiting for his name to be called to give his speech. After the Salutatorian and Co-Valedictorian spoke it was his turn. I saw his face turn down and his hands rub together in anticipation and nerve. His name was called and the blood flow in my body went faster and my heart skipped a beat every time he took a step closer and the smile that grew on my face became the facial expression of the night. I drew a breath in and I heard him speak.

The words that seemed to flow through his mouth and hit my soul, were anything short of wonderful. He talked of dreams, the ones who inspired him the most, the ones who he couldn't have gone on without, the goals they all should have when leaving high school. He spoke of many things and my brain seemed to tune it out. I heard the tone of his voice, the high and lows of his words, the smile that reached his face when he said something only he or I could understand and appreciate. I didn't know in that moment I could love and or be prouder of someone in my life. I didn't know I could be in love with the littlest thing as his voice. In the last words that ended his speech and the clapping that came to be, tears rolled down my face of how proud I was, and luckily enough it was my best friend and love. What couldn't be any better than this moment right now?

In that moment of thought my words were proven wrong. As I walked out into the arena area I searched for him through the hundreds of seeing eyes, scuffling feet, and prowl of those around me. In the moment I couldn't seem to find him and my hopes dropped, I picked out his tall figure and our eyes met. I didn't know quite what happened in that moment, but the dull embers of nerves faded from within and I felt his heart pull to mine. I felt in that moment strangely at ease. The shy smile of his grew wider and I knew that mine mimicked his exactly. I ran to him and I threw myself in his arms, his cap fluttered to the floor and the tears rolled down my cheeks as I felt his arms around me and the emotion of excitement for him fill my mind and heart. He slowly let me go and pushed me slightly away from him and the crooked smile he gave me made my night explode. The space between and around us filled with quiet and in that time, I tuned out everything around me.

"I'm so glad you came." He said to me with a huge smile on his face.

I smiled at him softly and I didn't know what to do or say, so all I did was kiss him harder than I had before. I smiled as we pulled away and he said that he should go find his family. I smiled as he wrapped his hand around mine and we went through the endless search for everyone in his family. I didn't even know I could be so happy talking to his family, seeing their faces, knowing how proud they were and I didn't even know I could be with someone who made so many people proud. He didn't gloat, he didn't have an exaggerated view of himself, he didn't need anyone to tell him different too. He somehow, humbly knew exactly what he could do but, in this knowing, it never got to his head.

His Mom and her family were planning on meeting up and I wanted to go with everything I had but my dad did not let me. As much as it irritated me I knew it was because we barely just started dating. So why get upset right?

BRRRRNGGG! BRRRRNG! BRNNNG!

I woke up to the sound of

my phone going off, and I couldn't possibly understand why someone was calling me at 8 in the morning on the weekend. My irritation dissipated as rolled over and I saw his name on the screen, my morning seemed to get better even if it was started early because it meant I could hear his voice. I was ready to start summer off because that meant I didn't have to do much and I got to see Spencer as much as I could. I reflected on the year and it seemed that I couldn't fathom how we were ever just best friends, but as I recollected all the memories, instances, and talks I knew that I didn't want it any other way, I knew that in some weird way it was supposed to happen the way it did. It was more than I thought I'd ever get to experience.

Chapter 10

I found that I didn't even know how to feel about us, not in any bad way but in an overwhelming way. I am happy, more than I thought I could ever be. The only reason for that is I didn't know after my previous relationship, I could find someone who not only I could love but honestly loved me. Where the fights, arguments, blame, no trust would finally end. I luckily got my wish and now my dream is a reality, and my reality is even better than my dreams before. This was into the first week of us dating and all I want is to be able to spend each day with him no matter what.

It has been officially a week since we started dating, May 27th. I don't know if I could ever explain exactly what I am feeling not only for him but in myself, true happiness is now a part of myself and I never knew what that felt like when I honestly loved someone the way I do for spencer. I could of course try and in writing in my journal, writing this, I only hope I can. The past week has been anything short of wonderful. Time has seemed to slip through my fingers and in the blink of an eye we have been out of school, he graduated, we got together. In the blink of an eye everything I have ever wanted with us happened, and I couldn't be more grateful. This week we have hung out a few times, I could say that everything is all honeymoon-stage, and like the fairytale romances in the movies but it is so much more than those. It is better.

Every time we hang out it is the most blissful time I have had in a long time with someone I cared about. We went to the movies, we hiked, we got food, we did all these normal things any person or couple does but with him it was different than with anyone else.

I didn't know how it felt to be honestly crazy about someone, I didn't know how I could ever feel as if my soul is on fire in the most beautiful ways. In the ways that when our eyes meet and I see everything I ever needed in his eyes it ignites all the deepest feelings any heart could possibly feel. Where your souls feel connected and not only together but as best friends before. I didn't know what it would feel like to look into someone's eyes and feel everything you ever hoped you would when you meet the one designed for you. It's rare, its chaotic, it's confusing, it's beautiful, it's achingly beautiful.

This feeling I hadn't felt before and honestly its more mesmerizing than I ever conjured up in my head. I have been cleaning, waiting for summer things, waiting for my birthday, I have been doing absolutely nothing. The weird thing about it, is that it felt better than before. I can say that talking to him, seeing him, hugging him can attain to the way I see my life now but it's much more. The way that I can just have him here is better than everything in between, and I remember as much as I can to tell him these feelings as often as I can. That he deserves from me and many others. So much more.

Dallas, Dallas, Dallas. It's a topic I have heard come out of his mouth for quite some time. He has been planning to go see his aunt in Dallas, which he is so ecstatic to do so. He is leaving the 16th of June and I'm happy but sad.

It was the early afternoon and Spencer and I were sitting and talking. The most exciting thing that happened right now as I looked into his eyes,

His face seemed to glow as he excitedly said, "I have big news. So, my stepdad has a few plane buddies who own part of a plane. Annnnnnnd, they are going to try to get me to be in it as well!"

I looked at him and I was surprised, ecstatic, outrageously happy. I jumped up into his arms and we both laughed at this newfound opportunity,

The joy that came upon his face as he knew this was happening was the most endearing expression,

I couldn't feel any prouder than in this moment.

He was going to learn, pick up things, and set up his career so early in his life and I couldn't contain he tears that filled my eyes and I put my hand on his face and whispered to him how proud I am.

His trip to Dallas was coming soon and I wasn't ready. He was going because he hasn't seen them in a long time and I am glad he is going to go see his family that he hasn't in a while. Although I am going to go to Santé Fe in a few days so I can't be too sad that he is leaving if I am going to as well.

Even still I know that I

am going to miss him like crazy and I believe he is going to miss me like crazy. We have been planning things for when we both come back which I'm glad for because I want to see him as soon as I can when I come back. We might be planning to go to breakfast, have a picnic, watch a movie, or go bowling we aren't sure which one we would like the most. I am leaving in a few days for Santé Fe and he has given me so many reasons to stay or just not stay that long and all of those are so I can see him a little bit longer before he leaves, it is the most endearing thing ever, and I appreciate how much he cares and wants to be with me.

Despite it all I am very excited to go down, we are

going to go to Chimayo which
is a very popular church down
there. We all wanted to visit
because we went there with our
aunt who passed away a few
years back so it is a very
cherished place for us to go.
From there we are going to go
to Safford and Silver City to
see our grandparents that we
haven't in quite some time. I
am going to miss him but I am
excited to see them.

The early glimmer of dusk
shone through my window as the
day began to finally start. I
found that twinkle of early
light amazing, it meant that I
was going on our road trip and
I couldn't wait for that. I

begrudgingly got out of bed and got ready for the 4-6 hour drive it was going to take. That was the only thing I was not looking forward too, besides, I get car sick very easily which I do not like much. I found myself excited for the trip but counting down the days till I got to see him again. I knew that would be the best day especially because he would be leaving soon too.

My mom, sister and I walked through stone arches that led to the most beautiful church. It was Chimayo and even though I haven't been much into church lately I still enjoyed it as much as I thought I was capable of.

It was the flowers, the arches the big willow trees and brick buildings. We stopped at a café and we got some food and ice cream, which my favorite part was. I could almost hear the chime of bells and rustle of flowers brushing against each other.

We got some rosaries, and some bracelets. So far it was a fun way to start off our girl's trip. We headed down to New Mexico to go see our grandparents and spend time with family. My cousins Zeik and Skylar came and it was so nice because I had not seen them in so long. We spent the time visiting, laughing catching up and eating delicious food. I was very excited to head back because his moms wedding was coming up on the 15th, but I am not completely sure that I can make it. I am hoping that I can but I know that it is not a huge deal if I do or not.

It was towards the end of June and he left on his road trip. I was very nervous for him drive all the way to Dallas but I knew he would be safe.

As this went running through my mind, my phone chimed with a message. It was from skype. I smiled because this meant I had another video from him. I felt my ease lift as I watched him talk about his night of driving, the wind turbines, the slight smirk on his face as he told me of how uncomfortable he was sleeping in his car.

He left yesterday but he stopped and slept through the night, so he sent me a Skype video in the morning. What that is, is ever since we became best friends he'd occasionally send me a skype video of him talking about his day, telling me what frustrated him and just talking to me. It was the sweetest, most thoughtful thing anyone has ever done for me. I occasionally send him some and it's just a thing that has always been part of our relationship.

Throughout the times at his aunts, I didn't hear a lot from him. I didn't mind in any moment because of the texts I would get late at night

"Oh, my gosh, I've had such a good time, did you see the video I sent? It was so funny Kat was dancing like that. George and I just have been playing video games, I just have missed them so much."

While receiving these snapchats, videos and pictures and texts it showed me just how happy he was to be there with family. His happiness made me happier than I could ever explain. As the week sped by like a train, and the anticipation of him coming back became reality, I couldn't wait for the moments like this, forever.

Chapter 11

The sun beat down on our faces
as we sat waiting for the
parade to start. It was July
3rd; our friends, Alex, Xavier,
Avery, my sister and I were
waiting for the parade to
start. It was hot beyond
belief but we were having a
good time. Spencer is meeting
us here and I can't wait. We
are planning to stay at the
parade for a little bit then
we are going to go hiking,
then eat. I'm very excited
because all my favorite people
are going and it's great. We
sat for a while and talked and
I got the text that I'd been
waiting for that Spencer was
almost there. Some of our
other friends started to show
up and coincidently Spencer
walked up I got so excited and

I immediately jumped in his arms. He laughed as I did and he squeezed me hard. I looked around at all our friends that were there, and I felt his hand in mine and it was the perfect moment.

I heard the breathlessness of everyone as we trekked down the trail. Not only was it hot, but it was a long hike that felt like walking up Mount Everest. We were not looking forward to such hardness. We took some breaks and we even stopped to just mess around, climb trees and knock some over. Any normal teenage things. We finally got to the spot where there were a ton of high rocks stacked and we all climbed up by a fallen down log. This was where the waterfall was supposed to be. As Spencer and I sat there, I sat further back from him and as we conversed with all our friends, I looked at him and the same exact feeling I had felt at the Grand Canyon came crashing in again but stronger. I smiled as I remembered the Grand Canyon and I went by him and I hugged him. My best friend, my future, sitting right next to me.

The smell of curry hit my nose as we walked up to the Taj Mahal and my excitement grew as we walked through the front doors. It was our first time being there but I was excited because I had never had Indian food before. We got sat down and we became excited for food. We ordered quite a few things, chicken masala, lamb, and a spinach dish, with a bowl of rice. We were going to divide amongst the whole group and I was excited. As the waft of curry and white rice steam hit my nose my stomach growled in anticipation. Spencer and I got ready to taste it at the same time,

As we both placed a spoonful into our mouths both of our eyebrows shot up. It was better than I thought it was going to be. When we finished I looked at the times for Finding Dory that we were going to watch. We quickly left the restaurant to head to the theater. We all sat next to each other in the perfect row, and as I placed my hand in Spencer's the movie started. It was honestly so cute and I am so glad we had decided to see it because its one of my favorites of this year.

The cadence of laughter filled the restaurant as my family and friends sat around for Sandra and I's birthday.

My sister, Sandra, she sat shyly but in the energetic nature of everyone's laughter she became more talkative. I found that this was perfect,

My family, my best love and parents, all my favorite people in one room. Spencer leaned into me, kissed me on the cheek and in an unexpected motion stuffed some pizza in my face. I laughed as I begrudgingly accepted the slice I didn't know I had.

The evening went on and as I ate some pizza, French macaroons and opened gifts it was beyond perfect. I glanced over to spencer and I saw him laughing and conversing, and it made me happier than I could have ever thought it could. I felt like this was the beginning of something even more beautiful than I ever imagined. I then asked my parents if it was fine if Spencer and I went out, they said it was okay so after dinner finished him and I walked out and we got to his car. I sat in the passenger seat and he asked if I could wait there and close my eyes. I closed my eyes and I felt something being placed on my lap. I opened my eyes and there was his beaming smile with his eyes squinted slightly, he said

"Here it isss!" He exclaimed as he set a cardboard box with multiple placements of tape.

I laughed loud as I held starting to open it. I found box within box. There was a mini tea kettle, The great Gatsby, my absolute favorite. There were watercolor art pencils, and a book. I looked at him as I pulled each one out and I smiled bigger than I thought I could ever do. I stood up and I hugged him tight and I grabbed his face I looked into his eyes and softly said,

"Thank you, thank you for being so great to me and knowing me, and always loving me."

With a grin on his face and he said,

"There is no one I would rather have in my life as my best friend, and love, all in one."

I smiled softly and kissed him, I just couldn't get enough of him. He was absolutely perfect.

We then headed to dairy queen to get some ice cream then back to my house. When we got there my parents were sitting on the couch and we conversed for a little bit and

It was honestly the best. I didn't know if anything could get any better than this.

The bang and echo of fireworks hit my ears and the bright explosion filled my eyes. It was beautiful, loud, chaotic. 4th of July has always been a good day, freedom, fun and most importantly fireworks and quality time. Sandra and I went over to our friend Alex's house with his dad and sister and it was so fun. We ate, talked and watched/ sent off some fireworks. I was beyond happy, I knew spencer wanted to spend it with me but we couldn't so I'm excited for the next time I can see him.

We left his house and when we got home it was just nice to get comfortable. Spencer called me and we talked until we both fell asleep. It was the perfect end to a great night.

I woke up slowly and started my day. Lazily even. I cleaned, laid around, wrote, honestly, I didn't know what to do so I decided to text him,

"Hey can we hang out today?"

I jumped in excitement as I saw his text that he would be free to hang out. July 7th about a week since my birthday and I missed him terribly. I eagerly got ready, and pretty soon he picked me up. I climbed into his car and I wrapped my arms around him and he hugged my waist tight and I never felt more safe or happy.

We pulled away and he looked at me so lovingly and softly kissed my forehead. I felt his hand in mine and as we went to the grocery store to get a few things for dinner today I could feel the happiness and excitement flow through my veins.

We stepped into the air-conditioned store and we shopped for ingredients for chicken alfredo rollups. We made sure every week to plan to do dinner and make sure it was something different. We finished at the grocery store and we took the 5 min drive back to his house.

We took out the groceries and carried them all into the house. I took each ingredient out and I started to prep for diner, they had to be in the oven for about 20 min so I wanted to make sure I was ready beforehand.

I looked over spencer's shoulder as he was shredding some mozzarella and I just smiled, I loved when we cooked together. It reminded me so much of when we became friends and got to cook together every day. I miss that. We finished prepping everything and we went and just relaxed till we had to put it in the oven, which is when his dad got home. I went over to the restroom and when I got out I just called out to him that I was going to lay down. I heard him turn on his x-box to play some video games and the next thing I knew I was waking up to sunset and Spencer lying next to me sleeping. When I looked over at him and the chilled evening sun rays that slowly were diminishing highlighted his face, I saw everything I ever needed.

I moved over to lay on his chest and as I heard the steady beat of his heart, I felt at ease in more ways than one. I pulled away from him and as we looked into each other eyes, our lips touched and the most magnificent thing happened. Before this, the kisses were always passionate, kind, loving but this time it was different, it was as if there was this hidden feeling that had fully come to surface. As our kisses molded and the dusk turned to night he kissed every inch of my skin, and unlike before I didn't hesitate. I felt the way our skin mingled and the electric pulse that came back through my veins as I kissed him. There was this new form of intimacy that I didn't know would change the spark between us so strongly. We met in the most physical, intimate, loving way possible. I didn't know what to think and, in this moment, I didn't want to begin to question it.

Intimacy has always been so foreign to me, but now it's exotic, passionate, connective, and truly beautiful. I suppose the most intimate moments I cherished now were the ones that I didn't ever want to speak about or get rid of. This

newfound level of intimacy
gave me a sense of truly
beautiful connections that not
all can speak about. Something
truly mysterious.

Chapter 12

Senior year, they hype of everyone's High School journey. A month away didn't seem long enough and I was bound on fixating my time on the few weeks that I had left in utter lazy.

The past 3 almost 4 months with Spencer didn't seem long enough but ironically enough it seemed even longer. I didn't know how to express the way being best friends with him for almost a year first helped us connect in a way I haven't ever experienced. I didn't know what this meant, and I didn't know this feeling but I never wanted it to stop. I was sad for the year to start but senior year I knew was going to be good, fun, new, and most of all, I wanted it to be over. I loved high school in some parts but it wasn't something I was going to miss much. I knew my life outside of it was going to be better, truly living. On an even more unrelated reason, all I wanted was more time with him. I wanted to live life completely transfixed in the moments with him in it, forever.

The warm wind blew my hair across my face as I reveled in the plane. Spencer was finally showing me the plane that he partly owns, its small, but utterly magnificent. Complicated especially in my eyes. Soon it didn't become complicated. He excitedly looked at me and said,

"Okay so this is it, and I get to ride in it whenever I want as soon as I get my pilots license, and this dial tells frequency, and this one controls rudders…"

As he went on, it seemed less complicated but still significantly confusing. I found my pride in him grow as his face lit up when he started talking about what he has to do and all the impressive things he has learned so far. I didn't know what else to do in that moment but look into his eyes as they lit up, and treasure him, completely. I honestly knew little about what he was telling me but he explained it slow and didn't keep going on if I didn't understand. He made me want to know and I didn't know that would ever be an option.

I smiled as he jumped out of the plane and bounced up and down smiling at me and he picked me up in happiness. As I heard the swoosh of wind in my ear and closed my eyes smiling at the smell of his skin, I didn't know I could be so proud of someone and be completely transfixed in their being.

BEEP! BEEEP! BEEEEP! I rolled over and begrudgingly hit snooze on my alarm and swung my legs over my bed. August

9th, it was the first day of school. It was utterly exciting and depressing at the same time. As much as I wanted to get school over with I wasn't ready to not see all my friends every day. I knew that I had to make the most of it but just get it done with so I could get on the next chapter of my life.

Sandra and I walked up to the school, it was too early but in spite of this we went to go see our friends to visit. It was strange to see them and know that it was our last year of high school together. I was glad that our group of friends were still together, it meant a lot for all of us. I went through that first day with anticipation and nerves. I met some new teachers that I liked more than a lot of others, I had class with some of my closest friends, the day couldn't have been any easier.

I got home that night and I was utterly happy, I knew that this year was going to go by good, fast, and blissful. I was ready.

About a month into school and it has been going better than I had expected. It has helped that I have been able to see Spencer, mostly when we are free and sometimes at lunch or when we are having an off day. We haven't been able to see each other a crazy amount but it's better than not at all. I am beyond excited because we are going to a play that is coming out at the college, Little women. I have read the book and he doesn't even know what it's about but we're super excited to go see it. We are just excited to see each other. We haven't been able to go on a date for a month or so and it has sucked. We needed it. We decided the day of the play we were going to spend as much of the day with each other as we could.

It was September already and I could feel the cool breeze that hit my face as I stepped out of work and got into Spencer's car. As we got into

Prescott we decided to go try a new restaurant we hadn't eaten at before. We decided on Al Gato Azul. It was really good and after that we headed over to the college to go to the play. We walked into the Performing arts center, high ceilings with chandeliers, and bright lights. We got into our seats and he looked at me with anticipation. I saw his smile brighten as the lights dimmed, I didn't know if life could be more perfect than having my person next to me as excited as I am.

As the stage light focused on the main scene playing out we were both smiling at how great it was. I remember how much I loved the book and seeing this reminded me of how much. As the intermission came, we both stretched as we got out of our seats, he looked at me and smiled. I looked at him and he asked if I wanted to go get something to drink, so we got some snacks and headed back over.

The roar of applause was thundering around us and the curtains closed.

It's been a month since the play and school has picked up but at the same time slowly been dragging on. Spencer and I have been seeing each other quite often but it doesn't seem like enough. I haven't seen him in a week or so because I've been hunting with my dad. I got drawn to go hunting and I was beyond excited. I already got one and this is the next day after I finally did.

The tv droned on and my grandparents and little cousins sat watching. The night seemed to be going well. That was cut short. A single text. A single text about a friend from high school. A single text that changed my hope in him.

Sara, Spencer, why?

Chapter 13

I felt my chest tighten and my irritation grow as I saw the words that popped out at me against the luminescent screen. My family and I were sitting at the couch watching tv and eating. I feared to tell them and bring up drama but it was eating away at me.

   "Spencer invited Sara to hang out with him at the house he is watching," the words blurted out and instantly I felt an ease.

   My mom and grandmas' eyes became large as they heard it. I chuckled at myself because of how ridiculous it sounded. It was not him. Surprisingly though, this is what I was dealing with.   They were friends in high school, middle school even, and that isn't what bothered me. They got in touch more because they saw each other because of college, I didn't mind much. They were friends, I knew that but she seemed not one to be trusted. He had girl friends from school and work except he had never invited one over at 9 o'clock at night.

Supposedly she was going through some stuff, like always it seemed, and she needed to get her mind off things and wanted to hang out. From the talks I have had with him this irritated him the most, how sad she seemed to be all the time.

I didn't know how to handle it, I didn't know how I could possibly not be a crazy girlfriend right now and tell him exactly what it made me feel like. In spite of those feelings I did exactly that,

"look I do have a problem with it. I just didn't want to bring it up and have an issue, but at night? Besides you are alone with her and I just don't trust that and It's not okay to do, imagine if I had done that?"

I hit send and anticipated what he would say, I didn't know what it would be but I didn't expect what he did say,

"ok yeah I understand."

It didn't seem like enough but I had to go to sleep for tomorrows party and I wasn't ready to worry about it.

I woke up with an aching feeling in my stomach, my mood was instantly turned upside down because of that. As we all got ready for the party, Spencer was going to meet us there and quite honestly, I didn't even know if I was ready to see him. Although we originally planned for him to go, so why fault ourselves for plans already made.

My family and I walked into peter piper pizza and the kids ran out of my grandparents hold and headed for the games. It was great to see, it was a party just for them. I came out of the bathroom from changing my cousin and I saw spencer standing there. I stopped for a split second and I didn't know what to do, cry or ask him to leave, I decided against both. As I walked up to him he reluctantly gave me a hug and we then set off to head into town. We walked to the car and it was an eerie silence that followed till I spoke up. I said hey, simple but groundbreaking. We decided to go eat and it was a great idea, we actually got groceries to make something and I was silently grateful, I wasn't feeling like being around too many people.

As we got to the house he was house sitting at, I automatically started making dinner. He looked at me confused, and slightly saddened. We usually did it together. We have every Friday ever since he graduated. I looked at him and I couldn't handle the unspoken hurt and tension, so I said

"Look I'm sorry for not seeming like I didn't trust you, it just baffled me and didn't seem okay but I do trust you."

He came up to me and put a hand on my face and slightly smiled and said,

"I probably would have done the same honestly."

I looked at him and sighed in relief. The rest of that night we talked about it. A slight tear slipped down my cheek as I set my face against his and I sighed out,

"I just don't want to lose you, ever. That's all I'm afraid of"

He grabbed my face and intensely looked into my eyes and his eyes etched with worry he whispered, "you'll never lose me, I promised you forever and I spent so long trying to find that and I'm not letting that go, nobody could ever take me from you, I promise you that always."

The tears were rolling down our cheeks as we pushed our foreheads together and I put up my pinky. I knew it was silly but pinky promises were always my and our thing. he smiled and put his pinky around mine, we then kissed our thumbs and pushed them together. We have been doing that since I could remember. Promising.

That night having dinner, it was blissful, I didn't feel that knot. I didn't feel tension, I felt love. In that moment I was even more thankful of the man he was, simply pure and perfect for me. In that moment all I knew is if a stupid girl wouldn't tear us apart, what could?

November 11th. A day that means more to us than any other. The day we fell in love with each other. The day I looked at him and saw my entire future, the day I looked at him and knew this was my forever person, my soul mate.

I trudged to his car, 4:00 in the morning not a time that everyone loves to be up and moving around. I sat down and I leaned over and kissed him softly. As we left to the Grand Canyon I fell asleep a few times. It was hard to because we were in his mom's Camaro and I was beyond excited to be in it. We stopped to eat breakfast and as the sunlight began to kiss the sky we made it to our spot. We sat there for an hour, watching the birds fly, throwing rocks, talking about life and everything in between.

As he laughed I saw that amazing smile of his and I was thrown back to that very first time I felt that feeling the first time. I knew in this life, in every moment, I couldn't find anything better. Nothing could ever take this perfect human from me and I knew it deep down to the core. He looked at me weirdly because I was staring at him with tears in my eyes. All I did was kiss him and tell him it was nothing, nothing at all.

When the weather seemed to become worse, it was cold, windy, almost unbearable we made our way to the nearby restaurant. It had comfort food and it was our favorite place to eat at.

We got sat in a spot by the window and as I looked at him, the sun hitting his face, while he sipped on his orange juice, I didn't know I could have someone like this. He was kind, loving, caring, he was everything, but so much more.

This year is ending, 2017 is

almost here. In this moment time didn't matter, school didn't, life didn't, he mattered and I never knew what that feeling felt like. I've been going through this year the happiest I have ever been and life with him seemed perfect, honest, loving, this life seemed practically untouchable.

Chapter 14

Christmas time, the time of the year that everyone loves. The cold brisk of morning and the way your breath hits the frosted air. The chime of Christmas melodies and the smell of Apple cider and cinnamon. Christmas has always been my favorite time of the year, I loved it always.

Spencer's favorite time was also Christmas and we were going to do our tradition of going to the courthouse lighting downtown. We have been doing it since we became best friends and we weren't going to let that tradition die.

I was getting ready to go out because we were going to

get downtown pretty early. I wore a red dress a green jacket and curled my hair. I knew it was going to be freezing. I was right too, as I stepped out of my house and saw him the wind whipped my hair around and it didn't matter much when he wrapped his arms around me in a warm cocoon. He looked so nice, nothing fancy on but just him. Dark jeans, tee-shirt, a jacket and black shoes. Just perfectly him. We drove downtown and it was super windy and cold, we immediately got hot chocolate, took pictures, looked at the things going on before the lighting and visited a ton of stores. It was perfect.

As the lights went out slowly in the stores, we stepped onto the sidewalk and one by one the trees, courthouse and sidewalks were lit with colors or red, green and orange. The twinkle of the lights that filled that night was magical. It was like the first time a year and half ago we went. It was perfectly amazing. I saw his face light up with joy as the falling lights turned on and I didn't know he could look more perfect in that moment. As we hugged each other watching the lights, reminiscent on our past and now our future, I felt my life flicker in front of my eyes, and it looked magnificent. He looked magnificent.

I felt my stomach knot up again for the 3rd time this month. She wouldn't go away, I didn't know why, I didn't know why he didn't stop it. He was hanging out with Sara a lot but the difference now is he didn't tell me anymore. I didn't know why, and this was the first time my trust started to waver, it started to diminish in slow flickers. He has been flying so much, going to Tucson, Cottonwood, Flagstaff, California, anywhere he could. I didn't know I could be so proud of someone this much but he seemed to make this happen every day. As much as I felt all of these things for him, this situation I could not understand. He wasn't telling me anymore, he was saying things to her that didn't sound right; for instance,

"I was literally thinking of you right now."

Perfectly innocent in his eyes but not in mine. This seemed to heighten more as she started to say things to him that was none of her business, things he never talked to her about but she stuck her nose in.

I read these messages one night we were together and I saw a message from her,

"Do you ever get worried about Sammi being in High School still?"

He replies, *"no why would I be?*

She then automatically responds,

"well she has a lot of guy friends and she has a picture

of one on her face book a lot."

He then says,

"No, I trust her and she doesn't spend a lot of time with them unless its school, I don't see the worry."

This was weird of her to state this when she knows nothing of me and especially our relationship. 1. The guy is my gay friend, and 2. It's really none of her business, especially when he has told me that they aren't that close anyway and they just talk when it's to her convenience, I have told him he needs to tell her to stop, and even she should know when to not budge into someone's relationship.

For me, this seemed

perfectly normal for a girlfriend to want when another girl is trying to get something from him. The difference these times is that he didn't say anything back to her. He didn't stick up for us, he didn't just ask her to stop talking about it. I didn't know why but I needed to know. I saw a text from her that was the last straw, she said that he should not trust me especially if they can't spend time alone together. Of course, I knew what she was doing but all he said was ok. I didn't understand why he couldn't just ask her to stop talking about it just to get out of our business because it wasn't her choice to say they should be alone whenever she saw fit.

This has been going on

since October, its March 14th now and I am just completely fed up. I then asked him if we could meet up, tomorrow to figure something out. Of course, he thought we were going to break up and he was not himself the rest of the night. I didn't know what to do about his thoughts until tomorrow but I just needed to leave it as it was.

I saw him and my heart dropped as I saw him sitting at a table with his head down. I walked up to him and he slowly looked at me and as he took off his sunglasses, I saw his eyes, pain filled them and they were slightly watery. My heart broke in that moment. I didn't care how much she caused problems, I didn't care in that moment that he never said anything, all that mattered was that he knew it was ok. The sunlight hit his green eyes perfectly and I laid it all out for him,

"look I trust you I do, but it's her, she just can't be speaking like that when it isn't any of her business. You never say anything and that hurts, you let her say whatever she wants about me and our relationship, that's not ok. Please I just want to figure this out."

He looked at me with angst in his eyes and he sighed and said,

"Yeah, I know you're right, I guess I just don't

want to start anything with her when I don't see the point because it doesn't matter anyways. I think you do also need to stop hanging out with Bradley."

I looked at him and didn't know what to say. Bradley has been my closest friend for a few years, he's the one in the photo Sara was talking about. I knew this would solve things as long as we compromised. So that's what I did even if it was hard for both of us to not hang out with our friends outside of school. It didn't matter much because Spencer did even more. I could do this because he was so much more.

I felt the relief go through my veins as we hugged each other. I felt the pain and fear leave his posture and I felt my worry and fear leave mine. I knew nothing could stop us even if it was someone wanting to try to jeopardize us. I knew now that nothing could tear us apart.

Graduation, it's the most anticipated time of the year, and it was today. I felt the anticipation as I was finishing my cap, getting my outfit together and steaming my gown. It all seemed too surreal, it was crazy but I was ready for it.

As I walked into the event center, I saw spencer walking towards me, I ran to him happier than ever before. I knew it couldn't get any better than this. I excitedly stood next to Sandra getting ready to walk out where everybody was waiting to receive our diplomas.

We sat there excitedly as the Salutatorian and Valedictorian finished their speeches and as we heard our names we walked across that stage. I felt ready, I felt excited, I felt grateful as I looked up at spencer and saw in his eyes my home.

As all my friends and family came to say congratulations I felt happier than I thought I ever could. In the car with spencer we headed to my house. It was a perfect end to my night, dinner, presents, dessert, and falling asleep in the arms of my perfect man.

18. 18 years old. 18.

Man 18 is the age that everyone hypes up and today I felt nothing different. The possibility of 18 excited me but the reality of change was neutral. I was excited more for our birthday celebrations with our friends and my Spenc.

Sandra and I walked out of the house and all our friends that were coming down to phoenix with us, Rosio, and Avery. I was beyond excited to head down. Spencer got in the driver seat, me in the passenger and the rest in the back. We were headed to the new Aquarium and we were beyond excited to see what they had there. I was excited for the butterfly exhibit that was there but I was more excited to spend the day with all of our friends.

Spenc and I walked through that exhibit in a childlike happiness. I saw his face, I saw everyone's and I was more than excited, I was content.

"Let's go!" I exclaimed to spencer. We had been wanting to go on a trip and he told me he has never been to Disneyland and I knew he had to. That is a place everyone should go to at least once in their lifetime. I knew he was going out of town for the end of July for Osh kosh. Airplane Fun for him, and I was so excited he was going to do that. I knew he was going to love it. We then planned to go the very end of July, July 31st was the plan till August 3rd because the first semester of college was starting and we wanted to get back. This was our very first trip we were beyond excited. This was the most excited I have ever been about a trip because he was there, right next to me 24 hours of the day for 4 days. How proud I was to be his.

Chapter 15

6 a.m. Not ready at all for being up this early. I slowly rolled out of bed and threw some comfy clothes on ready for a 6 ½ hour drive. As spencer pulled in and we packed our luggage, blankets and pillows up, I was now excited to start this trip. As we said our goodbyes we excitedly got in the car ready to get some snacks and hit the road.

We got to the grocery store and pigged out on all the snacks we craved for. I jumped up and down on our way to the car knowing this was officially when our road trip started. It was going to be long but oh so worth it. It was an hour in and its been probably the best hour on any road trip I've ever taken, we talked, laughed, sang, and just enjoyed each other and the scenery, we had 5 ½ hours to go. Far too long.

The smell of sea, and palm trees hit our noses as we came into Anaheim. I looked around me and I didn't want anything other than to get this trip started. We looked at each other and the smiles that spread across our faces was of pure anticipation. We pulled into our Hotel and got all checked in. He really wanted to see where Disneyland was so we could have our route all laid out. We struggled for a second to find the correct roads, but eventually found our way.

We made our way back to the hotel so we could get settled in and go get something to eat. He really wanted to take me to El Pollo Loco, I didn't mind what we ate, all I wanted was some food. When we pulled in we were excited to eat some hopefully good food, which we were correct about. As we sat at a tiny 2-person table with the lights of California behind him, and the luminescent glow of the restaurant lights, I grabbed his hand. I didn't want this to end, ever.

Another early morning that I wasn't ready for but knew meant Disneyland. The smile that came on his face as we walked hand in hand to the entrance. Even the excitement that came upon his face as we rode on the trolley there. It was magical just because of his reactions.

The park came into view and when we had stopped, we walked our way to the ticket booth. Tickets bought, backpacks on, smiles big, we made our way. We walked in got some pictures he jumped up and down a little as we walked our way up to the train on our way to New Orleans Square. We came upon the little town, all the amusements and restaurants. We went on the Haunted Mansion, Pirates of the Caribbean, a canoe ride, splash mountain, teacups, space mountain which was our absolute favorite. He wanted to go on it over and over again as well as splash mountain. While going through the park we passed the rides for Tarzan and the fire dancing shows, we came upon the stand for dole whip. It was dole whip with pineapple juice his favorite. We waited in anticipation for them to be ready and when we got them they were our favorite. We wanted buckets full of them.

It was severely hot but we didn't mind because we were having way too much fun at the park. We skipped around anytime we could, we kissed often and hugged frequently. We made our way to the huge stores in the front of the park and as I walked around and showed him all the things that he could get, all he wanted was a huge lollipop. I didn't know why but I didn't question, I just admired him as he reveled in all the choices. It was perfectly him, childlike, happy and amazingly perfect. We left the park sweaty, slightly overheated, sort of wet, and happy. As we got into the hotel room, he automatically passed out, I reveled in the amazing person sleeping next to me. Amazing, loving, perfect, just him.

I woke up to almost being off the bed as Spencer lay sprawled out as close to me as he could. I sighed in annoyance and rolled him over, even though he had been doing that since I could remember I didn't mind at all. I smiled as he woke up just as his alarm went off. He groaned, but we begrudgingly got ready to head out. As he got out of bed he walked over to his lollipop and stopped suddenly. I was very confused until he laughed, turned to me held out his lollipop and said,

"What the fuck even?"

He looked at me annoyed and all I could do was try to keep from bursting out laughing. I could see the round glint of sugar and the green mess of its melted consistency going down it.

He shrugged and looked disappointed as he threw it in the trash can. It was so bad but so funny. We put on our swimsuits and got ready to head out to the beach. We first stopped at Canes to get something to eat and then target. I needed a new top and he needed some shorts. Besides I loved shopping so any chance I could get I would take it.

We got some food and it was honestly the best chicken strips I've ever tasted. We excitedly drove to Newport Beach ready to find some seashells and enjoy the sea.

We both smiled as we looked at each other as the squish of damp sand fell between our toes and the sea mist hit our face at the most calming pace. It was magical, it was beautiful, it was more than I imagined with him. As we lay down our blankets and got out of our clothes in the shiver of bathing suits. We both smiled held hands and ran out to the ocean, laughing as the waves hit our legs. As we ran through I smiled as he was lowered down finding a shell, unknown to him that there was a huge wave crashing to him. I contemplated telling him but I knew it would be greater to see this play out.

I called out at the last second, "Babe!"

He looked back at me just as the roar of the wave came splashing down on his face. I laughed uncontrollably as he grinned at me and pushed me towards the next one. It was beyond bliss. I sat down on the blankets and he hurriedly came up to me dragging me to some rocks.

He looked at me and pointed,

"I found the jackpot of shells!"

I saw the excitement lift his face in a huge smile with his cheeks slightly pink from exertion. It was perfect as we sat picking shells, admiring each and every one. We went back and placed all of our shells in my hat and he jumped up and down and suggested we bury each other. I completely agreed with him and I laid down, I saw his face fill with laughter as I got covered more and more. He looked at me with a smirk on his face as he took a picture. I slowly got up and

there was sand everywhere.
Once he saw that he
begrudgingly laid down. I
covered him extra amounts and
as I took his picture he
slowly got up and sand
billowed everywhere. As I was
sitting down I was laughing
way too hard. I didn't want
that day to end but walking
hand in hand with him down the
beach basking in the beauty
and reveling in each other I
knew nothing could ever beat
this moment.

I rolled over and saw him
lying there peacefully. It was
our last day there, I saw a
peek of light come in and I
snuggled closer not wanting

this to end ever. The shriek of the alarm went off and we both slowly stretched not wanting to get up. We got our things together knowing there was a set time we had to check out. As we got everything in the car, I looked at the hotel reminiscing our first trip knowing that this was the first of many. He kissed my forehead as he opened the door for me and I got in the car, ready for the ride back.

We stopped by the Palm Springs Air Museum because his stepdad, Bob suggested it and he really wanted to go. I saw his excitement as we walked up and we made our way to the front desk they told us where everything was. We went upstairs and there was books, photographs a simulator which he fell in love with. The best part was as we went through the museum he talked to former pilots who worked there and he knew almost everything. It was impressive, in that moment, I was prouder of him than I have ever been. His excitement increased as he saw all of his favorite planes and he could check out a few of the insides of them out. Even though I knew nothing of planes, watching him enjoy it made me know it in a way I hadn't before.

We Left California after a few hours and as the scenery passed by and I listen to all the things he loved there, I stared at him and there couldn't be anything in the world that could ever change this moment.

The
Dim

Chapter 16

College. Going to Yavapai
College.

It was almost here I was
excited but slightly nervous
and worried. Spencer calmed
that nerve because I knew I
would get to see him all the
time, have classes, have
lunch, see him more frequently
than just on days off. I was
most excited to be able to see
him, that was going to be
worth it all. I had art,
communications, math, English,
and critical thinking. It was
going to be different but
good. Spenc had
communications, sociology,
computer systems, advanced
engraving and advanced
Aviation meteorology. He was
just ready to get this

semester over with. One more semester after this and he was going to be done with his second year of college. I was so proud. He is so impressive and I was ready to see where he was going to get in his career. We got ready for college as much as we didn't want to but was excited for.

A month in, it was exciting, easy and fairly amazing. I got to see him as much as I wanted, and we started to work out.

We have done so much since we first started. Going to the gym, him working a ton, him working more on his jeep, him flying more. He was doing so much and being there to witness the greatness that was him was worth everything to me. Laughing, loving, working out, eating, studying, falling. All of this was even more magical by his side.

We have had a small bump in the beginning of the semester but nothing we didn't work past right away. Bradley was going to college, and he didn't know honestly, I didn't know. That irked spencer and somehow that led to the irritation with me.

Finally, finally we laid it all out on the table. I said that this whole thing has been plain stupid and wrong in our relationship. He had sighed looked at me and agreed, he said "look nothing with him bothers me I just worry about you hanging out with him. Honestly, Sara is just someone who confides in me when she is upset which is literally all the time, I don't get it but I'm a friend to her."

As he voiced these thoughts I knew that this whole thing shouldn't have ever been a thing. We came to the agreement that this didn't really matter because our trust and love overrides it all and it's been nothing but dumb. As these threads of worry, stupidity, and overreaction dissipated so did the irritation. I had looked at his face and knew that I could get over anything as long as he was there. Perfectly there.

Dinner, working out, it was a perfect mix, right? We stepped into the gym, looked at each other and said,

"let's do this."

Working out has become our new love, and mostly because it was our thing to do together. We wanted to do something that would better ourselves and would become our thing. After working out he really wanted to get a haircut because he had been really needing to get one.

I showed the stylist the haircut that I wanted to give him, he looked at me skeptically but excited. As his hair slowly trickled down to the floor and slowly his haircut came into view I gasped. It was different, it was amazing, it was perfectly amazing. It suited him perfectly and I knew I was going to have to watch out for the girls that would now see how sincerely handsome he is.

Now dinner, that's what I honestly wanted to do, eat food. As the red luminescent lights hit his smile-stricken face I fell even more in love. We ordered mozzarella sticks and had chicken it was more than I could ask for that day since we couldn't do something the day of our anniversary date. We walked out into the slightly chilly night but the breeze came perfectly despite the chill. We sat there for hours talking, it was pure. As we sat he closed his eyes and rested his head on the headrest and as I admired his peaceful face I knew I couldn't ever lose him, I've always known but, in that moment, it hit me with the intensity that I hadn't ever experienced. I placed my hand on his face tears in my eyes and I told him that I could never ever lose him, he couldn't ever leave me because he was everything I ever needed. His eyes opened slowly and he smiled softly with a tear in his eyes and he said,

"I'm always here, I've always been here. I promised you that years ago and that is not changing, Forever, that promise is now until we can finally spend our lives together."

My heart seized and that feeling I felt 2 years ago sitting on that ledge with the sunrise hitting his face filled my angst.

My forever, seemed not too far away.

I woke up to the light beaming in my face and the chirp of birds. I lay in soft blankets and b cushions and I didn't want to get up but I knew I had to get my day started.

Math, math, math and Spencer. That is what my day

is consisting of. I knew as long as I got as much math I could the more time I would spend with him after he got off of work. I was pounding numbers in my hand and letting them fall out of my fingers hoping it would be right when I suddenly got a text from him that slightly disappointed me.

"Hey can we hang out tomorrow?"

I looked at it and my immediate reaction was no, all I wanted was to spend time with him especially when we haven't had time. It was the 21st and I just wanted to spend time since it was our anniversary date a few days ago. I knew though that he was going flying, he hadn't been in a week or so and he loved it so of course I said yes. I knew flying gave him joy and I would never take that away from him.

"Of course, just let me know when you leave please."

I heard the ring of my phone and his name popped up. As I said hello, I heard his voice, that sweet, shy, masculine, loving voice and I knew that I could wait a day to see him.

4:07

"Headed out baby, I love you, I'm in love with you."

6:30 p.m.

......

9:40 p.m.

......

11:42 p.m.

......

I texted him, multiple times, I didn't know why he wasn't answering me but my parents just thought rationally. He probably was eating, sleeping or maybe his phone died. I knew that that would be the only logical reason, I texted him goodnight, and that I just needed to hear from him. I needed to know he was okay

I went to bed that night my heart heavy, my stomach queasy and my mind frantic. This wasn't him and I knew somehow, I would hear from him. I just wished it was now.

Just tell me I'll wake up with
a text. Please.

Chapter 17

<u>Present day</u>

I sit here, almost 6 months later that I had started this book. This was the most dreadful part that I didn't want any part of. I knew it would come and now that I'm here, it sucks harder than ever. I didn't know if it all could be worth it, the loving, the confusion, the loving again, the heartache, oh the heartache. Would it be worth it all knowing the ending, although its hard could I be getting ahead of myself, knowing exactly what this gave me?

I needed this and all I know is that every painful type of my keyboard is worth it. The hardest time in my life now becomes your reading. It hurts, it tugs, its more than I can handle, but hopefully better for you. Hopefully.

I woke up at 5 in the morning with a tug in my heart, that I could only guess was the demise of the logic in my brain. Maybe it was the voice in my head and the tug in my heart telling me to find him. I didn't know what it meant but, I knew something wasn't right. I knew it but I couldn't know, and somehow, I didn't want to know until I heard from him. I looked at my phone and absolutely nothing.

I didn't freak out though, how could I possibly without context, but I just needed to wait till it was a more reasonable time in the day.

8:00 a.m.- "good morning you"

I sent it hoping I'd get something in a few hours, I knew he'd be up by then.

9:19

......

9:20

......

10:00

Nothing. Absolutely nothing. I knew now that something definitely wasn't right. This wasn't like him, this wasn't my Spenc.

My dad and I headed out to the airport to check if he was still there or if he wasn't, I just needed to know. As we pulled up to the gate, the gleam of his silver car that glinted back in my eyes like a flashlight became evident, became clear in my heart. His car was still here, what did that mean? Where was he? Did he land somewhere for fuel and stayed? Where did he go? All these questions in my head sped up the pace in my heart.

I called his mom to see where he was, I needed to know if she knew anything. I heard the worry in her voice as she told me

"Oh no, I didn't even know

he was flying, but it isn't right that his car is still there."

My stomach dropped as she told me she needed to call the sheriff now. My heart contracted as my worry began to take over. The tears spilled down my face as I went back home, I needed to get my thoughts together, I knew that. How could I though?

I walked into the house in a trance, I didn't know what to think. I just needed to know where he was. I needed to know he was safe. I needed the assurance, now. I needed him now and I didn't want to wait to have that.

I got the call from his mom that they were sending out the search party and were at the hangar. I needed to be there, I needed to know when they found them safe. Walking up to the hangar I immediately ran into his mom's arms. Her face was filled with worry and her eyes etched with tears and angst. My heart began to seize as my worst fears with him becoming a pilot ran through my mind. He was meticulous, careful, happy, I knew there wasn't anything he couldn't handle. I knew that he was safe, he always made sure.

11:00 a.m.

......

12:30 p.m.

......

1:00 p.m.

......

I sat on the edge of my seat clutching my moms' hand and the necklace we got together. The sheriff came in and I knew this was to either be good or bad news. I felt in my core it has to be good, how could it not? I saw his mom hug his stepdad Bob and I didn't know what it meant, they were in the other room. I didn't know what this meant at all.

She slowly walked in and I saw her face drop as she said,

"They're gone, Spencer and Jeremy didn't make it."

I felt the noise around me go mute, the lights seemed to dim and my stomach dropped and my heart shattered. I dropped to my knees shaking, aching, crying. All I can remember is saying "no."

This couldn't be. This couldn't happen. I felt my world spin as my mind couldn't register what this was, it couldn't be happening. He couldn't be gone. I can't be alone now. My heart seemed to fall out of my chest as I saw his face flash in my mind and my vision went blurry. I felt my heart seize and I remembered his face, voice and personality. I felt my body go numb. This isn't real life. What was this. This can't be anything real.

I sat in my bed, zombie-like.

My friends came over, hugged, laughed, cried, apologized. I called his friends, hesitant on Sara but knew he would want me to tell her. I heard Jacqui's, Larissa's, Cole's voice, I heard the ache, the heart break.

I hope I didn't sound like it but I knew I did.

What was this? I found my mind foggy as my friends talked. I found my ears close as they asked me how I was. My mouth didn't even feel like mine as I said I was handling it. I found my mind groggy as I tried to make sense of this all.

Most of all I felt my heart cave. It broke in pieces as my newfound emptiness poured its way in my cracks. The sound of heartache was haunting, I didn't like it. I didn't know what to do with it. It filled my ears as if I had headphones on with this treacherous song on, cemented on. It was my newfound skin, and I wanted everything to be able to rip it off and put my old one on but, how could I?

I didn't know what I was doing. I sat there entranced in my own thoughts. I didn't think this could be it. I didn't know this could ever be the end of us.

I wanted him here.

I needed him.

Forever with him was all I

needed, now it was a heartbreak away. In this moment I didn't know what to do, what did this mean for me? How was this my life now? How could I lose him so soon, how could this be my new reality? I didn't believe it, I didn't want to believe it, how could anyone?

Chapter 18

All I can say is, what do I do
now?

It's the end, how I applaud you for making it to the end when I couldn't even while writing it.

By now I would have liked to say that this was easy.

I would like to say that writing this gave me a freedom I couldn't find. It didn't, but what it did give me was hope.

It gave me hope in a blurry world of mine.

So,

You made it.

I made it.

-To you

I would like to thank my family for the needed support, and love

My friends, for the endless care and love through the worst times.

Spencer's parents for the support, love, understanding and welcome into their family.

Thank you to myself, for never giving up and persevering when I didn't want to.

Finally; thank you Spencer, for giving me light even in a world without you.

-Dedication

Samantha Rose-

An empathetic, funny, helpful, stubborn, imaginative, authentic, discerning, vivacious, beautiful young lady. Along with her twin sister adopted at 3 years old. Who graduated Chino Valley High-School, attending Yavapai college while pursuing and living her dreams,

Artist,

Interior Designer,

and an author,

Now through her darkest moments; a fighter.

-About the author

Made in the USA
Middletown, DE
25 September 2018